THE INCREDIBLE JOURNEY TO THE CENTER OF THE ATOM

W... *a journey like no other. Not simply a trip from place to place of the sort people make every day. This is a voyage from everything to almost nothing. From the unimaginably big to the incredibly small. From the Universe (which may be 100 million billion billion billion billion miles wide) to the particles which make up a single atom (perhaps smaller than one hundredth of a billion billionth of an inch across). As we travel from one to the other, different scenes come into focus. Let's find out what each one holds in store for us...*

BARNES & NOBLE
BOOKS
NEW YORK

UNIVERSE

IMAGINE *we could see the whole Universe laid out before us. It may look something like this illustration. (Measuring just over 10 inches wide, this disk represents an area billions upon billions of miles across!) There would be plenty of empty space, with clouds of misty light here and there, many linked together by thin wisps of cloud.*

Our journey takes us in towards one of these clouds. As we approach, we can see that it is made up of a cluster of thousands of lights. Then, as we zoom in towards just one of them, it becomes clear that the light is, itself, a cluster of 30 or so different points of light. As we get closer and closer, those points gradually take on shapes: spirals, spheres, or simply blobs.

One of those twinkling spirals is of particular interest to us. The next stage of our journey takes us in for a closer look.

POSSIBLE FATE OF THE UNIVERSE (1)

The Universe will keep on expanding forever

THE UNIVERSE MAY CONTAIN ABOUT 100 BILLION GALAXIES • THE UNIVERSE WAS NEARLY 20,000 MILLION DEGREES FAHRENHEIT

SECOND AFTER THE BIG BANG, THE TEMPERATURE OF THE UNIVERSE

UNIVERSE

THE UNIVERSE is everything we know—and much more besides. The vast stretches of outer space, stars, planets, moons, everything around you (and including yourself) are all part of the Universe.

Distances in the Universe are so vast we have to use a special measure to record them: the *light-year*, or the distance that light travels in one year (about 6,000,000,000 miles). The most distant objects we know in the Universe are calculated to be more than 13 billion light-years away!

Most of the Universe is just empty space, but scattered across it are billions of GALAXIES. These are enormous collections of stars, gas, and dust. They come in different shapes and sizes: Some are giant spheres, others magnificent spirals, still others irregular blobs. Galaxies are by no means evenly positioned in space. They tend to group together in clusters. For example, our own galaxy, the Milky Way, is part of a cluster of about 30 galaxies. Other clusters may contain thousands of galaxies. Clusters of galaxies, in turn, make up superclusters.

Many scientists think that the Universe was born in a colossal explosion called the BIG BANG. In this explosion, about 15 billion years ago, all matter, energy, space, and time were created. Such was the force of this explosion that, to this day, the Universe is still expanding. Gigantic clouds of dust and gas have clumped together over billions of years to produce galaxies, stars and planets—the Universe as we know it.

A NEARBY CLUSTER OF GALAXIES, CALLED VIRGO, CONTAINS AT LEAST 2,500 GALAXIES • A FRACTION OF A • SOME LARGE GALAXIES MAY HAVE MORE THAN 1,000 BILLION STARS •

THE UNIVERSE CONTAINS BILLIONS OF GALAXIES • THE UNIVERSE CONTAINS BILLIONS OF GALAXIES •

POSSIBLE FATE OF THE UNIVERSE (2)

The Universe will reach a maximum size and then contract: the "Big Crunch."

GALAXY

THIS *shimmering coil of stars and gas is our galaxy, known to us as the Milky Way. Somewhere, amongst all those billions of stars that form this dazzling catherine wheel in space, is our own star, the Sun.*

Looking down on the whole galaxy, measuring billions of miles across, we can see a swirling ocean of brilliant white studded with yellow, orange, red, and blue stars. At its center is a bulge, known as the nucleus. A number of arms uncoil from the nucleus, fading away into space in their outer reaches.

Our journey takes us down close to one of those spiral arms. The stars are all different colors and sizes. Some are colossal, measuring millions of miles across. And most of them lie billions of miles apart from one another. We are searching for just one average-sized yellow star...

IT WOULD TAKE A FURTHER 100 BILLION YEARS TO REACH THE FAR SIDE OF OUR GALAXY BY JET • OUR GALAXY IS ONE OF BILLIONS IN THE UNIVERSE • OUR GALAXY IS ONE OF BILLIONS IN THE UNIVERSE

IT WOULD TAKE 5 MILLION YEARS • IT WOULD TRAVEL BY JUMBO JET TO THE NEAREST STAR, PROXIMA CENTAURI, IT WOULD TAKE 5 MILLION YEARS • IF YOU COULD TRAVEL BY JUMBO JET TO THE NEAREST STAR, PROXIMA CENTAURI

BLACK HOLE

Cygnus X-1: gas from a giant star is gradually being dragged into a black hole

Cygnus X-1: gas from a giant star is gradually being dragged into a black hole

BLACK HOLE

GALAXY

GALAXY is the place in space where stars are found—in their billions. Every star you see in the night sky is part of the Milky Way, the galaxy to which our own star, the Sun, belongs (although on a clear night, you can glimpse one or two galaxies that lie beyond the Milky Way). Like our Sun, all these stars are giant spinning balls of hot, luminous gas, but they lie very much farther away from us. Almost certainly, many will have planets that orbit around them, perhaps some where there are living things.

Our galaxy, the Milky Way, is a spiral galaxy. It is named for the misty trail of stars across the night sky—our edge-on view of the galaxy. Seen from above, the arms of the spiral radiate out from the bulging center and contain young, bright stars. Our star, the Sun, lies on one of these spiral arms, about three-fifths of the way out from the center of the galaxy.

Stars come in different colors—according to how old they are. Blue stars are young and hot; red stars are old and cool. Orange and yellow stars (including the Sun) are young to middle-aged, and moderately hot.

Stars begin as clouds of dust and gas which collapse to form bright, hot cores. A medium-sized star, like our Sun, can glow brightly for billions of years. Eventually, it will use up all its fuel and swell into a giant. A very few giant stars finally explode (a supernova) before forming BLACK HOLES, regions of space so dense that nothing, not even light, can escape their GRAVITY. Many galaxies have a black hole at their centers.

A BLACK HOLE IS INCREDIBLY DENSE – EQUIVALENT TO A MARBLE WITH A MASS THE SAME AS PLANET EARTH • THE MILKY WAY GALAXY TAKES MORE THAN 200 MILLION YEARS TO COMPLETE ONE REVOLUTION •

OUR SOLAR SYSTEM LIES IN THE MILKY WAY GALAXY • OUR SOLAR SYSTEM LIES IN THE MILKY WAY GALAXY •

LIFE AND DEATH OF A STAR

1 Dense cloud of dust and gas forms
2 Dust and gas blown clear
3 Star and planets form
4 No change for millions of years
5 Star grows into red giant
6 Supernova or planetary nebula
7 Tiny, super-dense star

LIFE AND DEATH OF A STAR

SOLAR SYSTEM

A HUGE, fiery yellow ball floats in space. This is the Sun, our local star. Seen in our daytime skies on Earth, it brings light and warmth to our planet.

Circling counterclockwise around it is its family of planets. This illustration, showing all nine, is far from accurate in scale. The Sun's diameter is ten times bigger than that of the largest planet, Jupiter, itself more than eleven times wider than the Earth. Mercury, the nearest planet, lies 36 million miles from the Sun.

The orbit of each planet is shown here in a different color. In order from the Sun they are: Mercury, Venus, Earth, Mars, Jupiter, Saturn, Uranus, Neptune, and Pluto. The belt between Mars and Jupiter is made up of thousands of rocky fragments, known as the asteroids.

Next stop on the journey: Planet Earth, 93 million miles from the Sun.

MORE THAN ONE MILLION EARTHS COULD FIT INSIDE THE SUN • THE MOON IS LARGER THAN BOTH MERCURY AND PLUTO •

THE SUN IS A BALL OF EXTREMELY HOT GAS

◄ Arches of glowing gas rise from the surface

Jupiter and Earth are shown to scale ►

JUPITER'S 16 MOONS IS LARGER THAN BOTH MERCURY AND PLUTO

THE SUN IS ONE OF BILLIONS OF STARS IN THE MILKY WAY • THE SUN IS ONE OF BILLIONS OF STARS IN THE MILKY WAY

THE LARGEST OF JUPITER'S 16 MOONS

THE LARGEST PLANET IS 27 MILLION °F AT ITS CENTER •

THE SUN IS A BALL OF EXTREMELY HOT GAS

SOLAR SYSTEM

T HE SOLAR SYSTEM consists of the Sun and the nine planets (including our Earth), their 61 moons, COMETS, ASTEROIDS and gas and dust that all circle around it. The Sun is a star, very much larger than any of the planets. But it is just one of billions of stars in the Milky Way GALAXY, itself one of billions of galaxies in the Universe.

Unlike stars, planets do not produce heat or light of their own. The four planets closest to the Sun — Mercury, Venus, Earth, and Mars — are small and rocky. Next come the four gas giants — Jupiter, Saturn, Uranus, and Neptune — so-called because they each have huge layers of gas wrapped around their small, solid cores. All have rings, but Saturn's are by far the largest and most spectacular. The rings are made up of billions of rock and ice particles. Beyond Neptune lies Pluto, the coldest and outermost planet. It is much smaller and made of mainly ice and rock.

Like most stars, the Sun is a huge, luminous ball of hot gas. Inside, it is like a massive power station, where the process of *nuclear fusion* releases enormous amounts of energy (PARTICLE) which we on Earth see as light and feel as warmth. The Sun's surface bubbles and spits, sometimes producing arches of glowing gas called *prominences*. Sunspots are darker, cooler blotches on the Sun's surface.

A comet is a ball of ice that may have come from beyond Pluto. It is drawn towards the Sun by the pull of GRAVITY. As it approaches, it begins to melt and forms a bright head of gas which trails a long tail of dust and gas.

THE THIRD PLANET FROM THE SUN IS EARTH • THE THIRD PLANET FROM THE SUN IS EARTH •

...ART OF PLUTO'S ORBIT LIES WITHIN THAT OF NEPTUNE • JUPITER, SATURN, URANUS, AND NEPTUNE HAVE ALL BEEN PHOTOGRAPHED IN DETAIL BY THE SPACE PROBE VOYAGER 2 • THE SUN

THE OUTER SOLAR SYSTEM • A comet's orbit: pale orange •

Pluto's orbit: pale blue • Pluto's orbit: pale green • Neptune's orbit: pink • Uranus' orbit: pink • Saturn's orbit: orange • Jupiter's orbit: yellow •

THE OUTER SOLAR SYSTEM

EARTH

SEEN from space, the Earth looks like a giant, colorful marble. It is mostly blue (the oceans), with markings of browns, yellows, and greens (the continents) and streaks of white (clouds). Both top and bottom are also capped by white (the ice-covered poles). The clouds swirling around the Earth sometimes obscure, sometimes reveal the land shapes below.

There could not be a greater contrast than with another ball lying quite close by, about a quarter of the Earth's size: the Moon. This barren world is a uniformly dull grayish-brown and pockmarked with craters.

One of a number of man-made satellites circling the Earth, the Hubble Space Telescope, shown in the illustration, is used to observe the distant stars and galaxies.

As we move closer to Earth, we can start to make out more detail on the surface...

THE TEMPERATURE AT THE EARTH'S CORE IS THOUGHT TO BE ABOUT 9000° F • THE EARTH IS ONE PLANET IN THE SOLAR SYSTEM • THE EARTH IS ONE PLANET IN THE SOLAR SYSTEM • SLIGHTLY AT THE EQUATOR • IT BULGES • THE EARTH IS NOT A PERFECT SPHERE: IT BULGES • EARTH •

INSIDE THE EARTH

Plates moving apart ▲

Mantle

Mid-ocean ridge

Inner Core

Outer core

Convection currents

Mantle

Volcano

Plates are moved by convection currents, heat rising and falling in the mantle

◀ One plate sliding beneath another

INSIDE THE EARTH

EARTH

EARTH IS THE THIRD nearest planet to the Sun. Of the nine planets, it is the only one which supports life. Because of its position relative to the Sun, it is neither too hot nor too cold for the existence of liquid water, essential to life.

The Earth is surrounded by a layer of gas—its ATMOSPHERE. This consists mostly of nitrogen and oxygen, with some carbon dioxide and water vapor. It is thin enough to let through sunlight but sufficiently thick to block most harmful RADIATION such as ultraviolet light. The atmosphere also acts like a blanket, keeping the planet at an almost even temperature, and it provides the air that animals breathe.

The Moon, by contrast, lacks both an atmosphere and water. Consequently its surface temperature is always extremely cold and there is no life.

Like a peach, the Earth has a solid center. Its "stone" is the core, a hot ball of iron surrounded by liquid metal. Around the core lies the MANTLE, a thick, mostly solid layer.

The Earth's crust, its rigid surface layer, is made of several slabs, called TECTONIC PLATES which fit together like the pieces of a jigsaw puzzle. The plates float on top of the mantle and are always on the move powered by CONVECTION CURRENTS (heat circulating through the mantle). Where the plates collide or rub together they cause earth-quakes and fold the crust into mountains. Where they move apart or slip under one another, molten rock, or magma, from the man-tle rises to the surface through volcanoes.

THE SAME SIDE OF THE MOON ALWAYS FACES THE

OCEANS AND CONTINENTS MAKE UP THE EARTH'S SURFACE • OCEANS AND CONTINENTS MAKE UP THE EARTH'S SURFACE

LIGHT LEAVING THE SUN TAKES OVER EIGHT MINUTES TO REACH THE EARTH

THE EARTH TAKES 365.26 DAYS TO ORBIT THE SUN

THE EARTH'S CRUST IS DIVIDED INTO GREAT PLATES

Plate boundaries shown in red

THE EARTH'S CRUST IS DIVIDED INTO GREAT PLATES

Plate boundaries shown in red

LAND

STILL tens of thousands of feet above the Earth, we can now see its mountain ranges, valleys and plains, and the incredibly intricate pattern of rivers that snake across the landscape. Darker green textures indicate forests, while browns and grays signify bare mountaintops, here and there daubed with white snowcaps. The ocean is, of course, a deep blue.

The mark of humans on the surface of the Earth is clear to see. Across the lowlands lie swathes of golds and greens, the colors of crops growing in fields. The splashes of gray are the places where most people live: towns and cities. Some rivers have very straight courses: these are canals, built to channel water across fields, and to reduce the risk of floods.

Another product of human ingenuity sweeps by beneath us: a jet airplane.

THE VOLCANIC ERUPTION AT KRAKATOA IN INDONESIA IN 1883 PRODUCED GIANT OCEAN WAVES WHICH TRAVELED HALFWAY ROUND THE WORLD

OCEANS AND CONTINENTS MAKE UP THE EARTH'S SURFACE • OCEANS AND CONTINENTS MAKE UP THE EARTH'S SURFACE • OCEANS AND CONTINENTS MAKE UP THE EARTH'S SURFACE

THE AMAZON RIVER CARRIES ONE-FIFTH OF ALL THE WORLD'S FRESH WATER

THE WATER CYCLE

Water evaporates from the sea (and land)

Clouds, masses of condensed water vapor, form

Water droplets in clouds fall as rain (or snow)

Water runs off the land into lakes and rivers

The rivers empty their water into the sea

THE WATER CYCLE

LAND

THE SURFACE LAYER of the Earth, the crust, is made of rock just a few miles thick. More than two-thirds of it lies beneath the oceans. the rest makes up the land—the continents and islands.

Three types of rock are found in the Earth's crust. *Igneous rocks,* such as granite, form when melted rock (magma) rises to the surface though volcanes, cools, and solidifies. *Sedimentary rocks,* such as limestone, form when rock particles, sometimes including plant and animal remains, are compressed and cemented together. *Metamorphic rocks,* such as marble, are formed when igneous or sedimentary rocks are altered by high temperatures and pressures underground.

Water evaporating from the Earth's surface rises to form clouds, releasing rain (or snow) which falls back to Earth. The circulation of water plays a major role in shaping the land: Water and ice can wear down, or erode, all types of rock. For example, rainfall dislodges loose particles and rainwater may dissolve chemicals in rocks. When water is trapped inside cracks in the rock and freezes, it expands and splits the surrounding rock. Over thousands of years, rivers cut through rock on land as they make wider and wider valleys. In cold regions, rivers of ice called glaciers gouge out deep mountain valleys.

The eroded rock particles eventually become sediments, washed into rivers, lakes and the sea. Millions of years later they will be compacted back into rock, and the cycle begins again.

THE DEEPEST PART OF THE OCEAN IS THE MARIANA S TRENCH IN THE PACIFIC WHICH PLUNGES NEARLY 7 MILES BELOW SEA LEVEL

THE WORLD'S TEN HIGHEST PEAKS

LIFE IS FOUND NEARLY EVERYWHERE ON EARTH • LIFE IS FOUND NEARLY EVERYWHERE ON EARTH • LIFE IS FOUND NEARLY EVERYWHERE ON EARTH

THE HIMALAYA-KARAKORAM MOUNTAIN RANGE CONTAINS THE WORLD'S

THE ROCK CYCLE

THE ROCK CYCLE

Eroded rock particles are carried away by water

Igneous rocks form as melted volcanic rock cools

The particles accumulate as sediments

Metamorphic rocks form deep underground

They are compressed to form sedimentary rocks

ENVIRONMENT

OUR journey takes us closer still to the surface of the planet. A few hundred feet from the ground and we are joined by other forms of life: birds, masters of the air. The scene now is unmistakably the work of humans: crop fields are spread across the land like a patchwork quilt, while tracks and roads criss-cross between them. Dotted about are a few buildings and farmhouses, identifiable by their red roofs.

The less regular designs of nature interrupt this engineered landscape. A river winds this way and that across the fields, and clumps of woodland survive amid the geometric field patterns.

The scene is like a map of our surroundings. It is a picture of our own world at a scale we can easily understand.

DAYTIME SURFACE TEMPERATURES IN HOT DESERTS MAY EXCEED 190 · DIFFERENT ENVIRONMENTS MAKE UP THE LANDSCAPE · DIFFERENT ENVIRONMENTS MAKE UP THE LANDSCAPE · ANTARCTICA IS THE COLDEST PLACE ON EARTH: TEMPERATURES CAN BE AS LOW AS -126°F · THE LARGEST HOT DESERT IS THE SAHARA · 'S SURFACE

WORLD ENVIRONMENTS (1)

Desert

Tropical rain forest

Savannah (open grassland with trees)

Oceans

Coastal

Wetlands

WORLD ENVIRONMENTS (1)

ENVIRONMENT

THE ENVIRONMENT, our surroundings, includes the ATMOSPHERE, the continents, the oceans, and the living things that inhabit them.

Living organisms live in COMMUNITIES. These are collections of animals and plants that live in the same place and depend upon one another for their survival. The plants provide food for animals which, in turn, are eaten by other animals. Smaller ORGANISMS break down animal and plant waste (☞ SOIL), so releasing NUTRIENTS which plants can use.

The climate and physical landscape, including the nature of the underlying rock, determine the type of soil and the kinds of plants that can live in that area. The plant life, in turn, determines the types of animals that can thrive. Our world has many different climates and physical landscapes, so there are many different types of environment. Deserts, rain forests, or grasslands, for example, each have their own distinctive communities.

In a woodland community, many kinds of insects, spiders, and other small animals live in the trees or on the ground below. Various birds and mammals feed on these animals and they, in turn, may be preyed upon by other animals, such as birds of prey.

Human activities such as farming, city-building, and industrial manufacturing have drastically altered the natural environment. In many parts of the world, the appearance of the countryside and the kinds of animals and plants that live there are the result of human activities.

DESERT OCCUPIES ABOUT ONE-THIRD OF THE

THE SOIL IS ESSENTIAL TO LIFE ON LAND • THE SOIL IS ESSENTIAL TO LIFE ON LAND • THE SOIL IS ESSENTIAL TO LIFE ON LAND

OVER HALF OF THE WORLD'S TROPICAL RAIN FOREST HAS ALREADY BEEN CUT DOWN

OVER HALF OF ALL LIVING SPECIES IN THE WORLD

TROPICAL RAIN FORESTS ARE HOME TO ABOUT HALF OF ALL LIVING SPECIES IN THE WORLD

WORLD ENVIRONMENTS (2)

Tundra (treeless region south of Arctic)

Boreal (northern coniferous forest)

Polar

Mountain

WORLD ENVIRONMENTS (2)

Freshwater rivers

Temperate woodland

SOIL

WE are now just a few inches above the ground, face to face with animals that live in the soil. In this corner of the countryside, we are once again in the disordered realm of nature, Here are flowers and plants, fungi (like these beautiful red toadstools), fallen leaves and twigs. Living amongst them are animals of all kinds: mammals like the mole and the shrew; insects such as ants, beetles and flies; spiders, slugs and snails, earthworms, centipedes, and lice.

The soil is alive with activity, with all these creatures going about their daily lives. Some animals burrow down into the soil, while others are pushing up to the surface. Some bustle about in search of food, while others remain motionless, awaiting their opportunity.

Our next destination is a mysterious, close encounter...

A PLANT'S FOOD IS MADE IN ITS LEAVES BY PHOTOSYNTHESIS 1 Carbon dioxide (CO₂) is taken in from the air 2 Water is taken up from the soil 3 Sunlight provides energy 4 Sugars are made in the leaves from a reaction between CO₂ and water 5 This food is transported to all parts of the plant

LIVING IN ONE SQUARE MILE OF SOIL WILL BE ABOUT 600 MILLION A HALF PROTOZOANS (SINGLE-CELLED ORGANISMS) • OVER HALF CONTAIN MAY SOIL DAMP OF TEASPOONFUL HEAPED ONE • SOIL IS A VITAL PART OF ALL LAND ENVIRONMENTS • SOIL IS A VITAL PART OF ALL LAND ENVIRONMENTS •

SOIL

SOIL IS A MIXTURE of tiny rock particles and humus—plant material that is in the process of decaying. Between the particles are large air spaces. These are important because they allow water to drain through the soil. They also allow oxygen to reach both the plant roots and the ORGANISMS (living things) that inhabit the soil.

Plants use soil to anchor their roots. They take up water from the soil and transport it via the stem to the leaves. Using the energy from sunlight, plants combine water with carbon dioxide gas taken in from the air to form food—a process called PHOTOSYNTHESIS. Most land animals feed on organisms that grow or live in the soil, either directly, or when they eat other animals that do so.

A handful of soil may not look very exciting. But it is like a giant factory where a mass of tiny organisms, most of which are too tiny to see with the naked eye, are working away recycling the remains of dead animals and plants into NUTRIENTS. These are in turn taken up by the roots of living plants. The tiniest of the "workers" are called BACTERIA. That handful of soil will contain over *10 billion* of them!

Microscopic organisms made of only one cell, called *protozoans,* feed on bacteria, while they are themselves eaten by larger animals such as worms. Earthworms also have a vital role to play tunneling through the soil, letting air in, helping water drain through and mixing the different soil layers. Insects, spiders, and centipedes hunt in the soil, and larger animals like moles and voles make their burrows there.

IT TAKES ABOUT 10,000 YEARS FOR A MATURE SOIL TO FORM OVER UNDERLYING ROCK • MANY TINY FORMS OF LIFE ARE FOUND IN SOIL • MANY TINY FORMS OF LIFE ARE FOUND IN SOIL • EARTHWORMS IN A SMALL FIELD WILL SWALLOW SEVERAL TONS OF SOIL EACH YEAR • MILLION SPIDERS

VITAL CYCLES

Animals feed on plants growing in the soil

Waste, dead animals and plants decay

Tiny organisms turn remains into nutrients

Nutrients are released and taken up by plants

VITAL CYCLES

ANIMAL

THIS is a field tiger beetle. It is only a few tenths of an inch long but this illustration shows how big it might look to a passing fly. Glossy, emerald green with near-symmetrical yellow markings, this creature is a miracle of natural engineering in miniature. The beetle has six legs (each with tiny hooks for feet) and three parts to its body: the head, the thorax (its middle section) and abdomen (the rest of its body).

Two long, rodlike antennae project from its head just in front of its giant, bulbous, golden eyes. The antennae wave around in what seems like a random fashion, constantly probing the ground ahead. Below the fearsome jaws, smaller mouthparts twitch menacingly, slavering for a meal.

For the next stage of our journey, we enter the microscopic world for the first time...

THERE ARE HUMAN BEINGS • MANY SMALL ANIMALS ARE FOUND IN THE SOIL • MANY SMALL ANIMALS ARE FOUND IN THE SOIL • THERE ARE PROBABLY ONE MILLION TIMES MORE INSECTS ON THE PLANET THAN SEVERAL THOUSAND NEW KINDS OF INSECT ARE DISCOVERED EACH YEAR

LIFE CYCLE OF THE FIELD TIGER BEETLE

Adults mate to produce offspring

An adult emerges from the pupa in spring

Eggs are laid singly in the soil

A larva hatches from the egg and grows

The mature larva changes into a pupa

LIFE CYCLE OF THE FIELD TIGER BEETLE

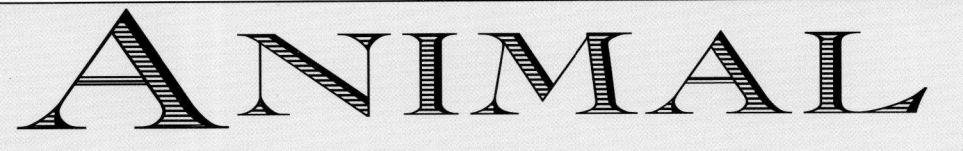

ANIMAL

OVER TWO MILLION KINDS of animal live on Planet Earth. They range
in size from microscopic forms to giants such as the blue whale, which can
weigh 160 tons or so. There are so many microscopic animals that they
are estimated to account for more than half the weight of all the world's
living creatures. About half of all *kinds* of animals are insects—small,
land-living creatures coated in a smooth, shiny, armorlike skeleton.
Beetles are the most abundant kind of insect.

One key difference between animals and plants is the way
they feed. Most plants take in simple chemicals from the soil
and air, and use sunlight energy to convert these into food
substances (☞ SOIL). Animals, on the other hand, obtain
their food by eating plants or other animals. Once
swallowed, the food is broken down (digested) then
distributed around the body by a transport system,
usually a system of tubes containing blood powered
by a beating heart. The food substances are either
chemically altered and used to construct body
parts, or broken down – with the help of oxygen
the animal has breathed in – to release energy.
Waste products are removed (excreted) from the
animal's body.

An animal's eyes, ears, and other sense organs
detect features of its surroundings and help the
animal find its food. A nervous system delivers
information from the sense organs to the brain,
which then sends messages to the muscles to
control body movement.

INTERNAL ORGANS OF AN INSECT • Red: blood system • Turquoise: nervous system (part of) • Brown: digestive system • Yellow: breathing system • INTERNAL ORGANS OF AN INSECT • Blue: reproductive system

THE TOTAL WEIGHT OF INSECTS IS OVER TEN TIMES THE WEIGHT OF ALL PEOPLE ON THE PLANET • ALL ANIMALS ARE MADE UP FROM CELLS • ALL ANIMALS ARE MADE UP FROM CELLS • ALL ANIMALS ARE MADE UP FROM CELLS • AN INSECT BREATHES THROUGH A SERIES OF TINY HOLES ALONG THE SIDES OF ITS BODY

CELL

WE are shrinking rapidly. Down into the beetle's leg, beneath the hard layer of its external skeleton, we arrive in an amazing new world. This illustration is of an area measuring just a few ten thousandths of an inch across. Here, there is a definite pattern. The "wall" before us seems to be made up of "bricks" each containing a similar variety of shapes. These "bricks" are cells, from which all living things are built. Each cell is surrounded by an outer skin. Inside, it is filled with a jellolike mass (shown in blue) with various tubes and globules drifting around. At the center lies a large gray mass: the nucleus.

Our journey takes us through the tiny holes in the nucleus' protective coat. Inside, we find tangles of threadlike material, called chromosomes. Let's shrink some more to see what they look like in closer detail.

CELL

THE SMALLEST CELLS BELONG TO BACTERIA, SIMPLE SINGLE-CELLED ORGANISM • THE SMALLEST CELLS BELONG TO BACTERIA, SIMPLE SINGLE-CELLED ORGANISM • THE SIZE OF A PERIOD • IT IS ABOUT THE SIZE OF A PERIOD • THE LARGEST CELLS IN THE HUMAN BODY

CELLS ARE THE BUILDING BLOCKS OF LIFE • CELLS ARE THE BUILDING BLOCKS OF LIFE • CELLS ARE THE BUILDING BLOCKS OF LIFE

THE EGG CELL IS ONE OF THE LARGEST CELLS IN THE HUMAN BODY

BILLION CELLS IN THE HUMAN BODY

AN ORGANISM GROWS BY CELL DIVISION

1 Chromosomes, containing DNA, are located in the nucleus 2 Each chromosome splits in two 3 Two cell nuclei are formed 4 The cell divides with identical DNA contained in each cell

AN ORGANISM GROWS BY CELL DIVISION

CELL

MOST PLANTS AND ANIMALS contain millions, sometimes even billions of CELLS. Each cell is microscopic in size, but they combine to form all body parts. The cells are the building blocks of the body, in the same way that bricks fit together to make buildings. Cells, however, come in many different shapes and sizes.

Every cell is surrounded by a thin, filterlike barrier, a cell membrane. This controls which substances enter or leave the cell. Inside the membrane, there is a mass of jello with various parts suspended in it. The cell is like a factory where some chemicals are broken down and others built up. Sausage-shaped structures called *mitochondria* (shown in red in this illustration) provide the "power." Other structures form mazes of tubes through which chemicals are transported around the cell. Still others make substances which are released into the surroundings. The cells in this illustration, for example, make the chemical *chitin* which forms part of the insect's tough outer coat.

The nucleus, the region in the center (shown here as grey), is like the computer program which runs the cell. It contains tiny threadlike bodies called CHROMOSOMES, into which DNA is tightly wound. Most animals and plants begin life as a single, fertilized egg cell. For the ORGANISM to grow, the cell has to divide and divide again many times over. The chromosomes split in two each time, so, as the organism grows, all its cells contain identical DNA.

THERE ARE OVER TEN THOUSAND SMALLEST STRUCTURES IN THE CELL • MICROSCOPES THAT MAGNIFY OVER HALF A MILLION TIMES ARE USED TO SEE THE

THE NUCLEUS OF A CELL CONTAINS DNA • THE NUCLEUS OF A CELL CONTAINS DNA • THE NUCLEUS OF A CELL CONTAINS DNA

SOME NERVE CELLS IN A GIRAFFE'S NECK ARE OVER SIX FEET LONG •

AN INSECT, FROM EGG TO BIRTH

1 A sperm from the male fuses with a female's egg 2 The nucleus of the resulting cell divides many times 3 The nuclei move outwards to form a layer of cells 4 The cells begin to arrange themselves into the body of the larva

AN INSECT, FROM EGG TO BIRTH

DNA

T HE chromosome threads are made of still tinier threads wound tightly together like the filament in a light bulb. And if you look closely at these tiny threads, you'll see that they themselves are also made up of two strands, each twisted around the other in a spiral. In this illustration, you can clearly see the two strands weaving in and out of each other. You can also see that the two strands are knitted together by countless cross-links.

These spiral strands make up the chemical known as DNA. It is a very special substance because it controls every cell in every living thing.

Look closely at the strands and you will see that they are made of what look like beads, all closely packed together. Those beads are atoms, the building blocks of all matter. Already we can see that there are many different sorts. Our journey takes us in to examine a group of them.

THERE IS ENOUGH DNA IN A HUMAN CELL HAS ABOUT SIX FEET • DNA IS FOUND IN THE NUCLEUS OF A CELL • DNA IS FOUND IN THE NUCLEUS OF A CELL • EACH CELL OF A FRUITFLY CONTAINS ABOUT 4 INCHES OF DNA; A HUMAN CELL HAS ABOUT SIX FEET • A DNA MOLECULE MAY CONTAIN OVER 1000 MILLION ATOMS

HOW DNA IS FOLDED UP INTO CHROMOSOMES

▼ DNA consists of two spirals linked by chemical bridges

Chromosomes are made up of loops of chromatin fibers

▼ Chromatin fibers consist of coils of DNA strands wrapped around protein molecules

▼ HOW DNA IS FOLDED UP INTO CHROMOSOMES

DNA

DNA (short for **D**eoxyribo**N**ucleic **A**cid) is a giant MOLECULE found in the nucleus of CELLS. Enormously long and complex, it contains the instructions for building and maintaining the cell. Since most cells in the body of a plant or animal contain identical DNA, this chemical contains the instructions for building the entire bodies of plants and animals.

The DNA molecule is like a long, spiral ladder, sometimes called a double helix. The two twisted "uprights" of the ladder are linked together by chemical bridges that form the "rungs." These chemical bridges are of four kinds. The exact order in which they appear on the ladder is like a code.

A GENE is a short section of DNA. The code sequences in genes carry instructions for making PROTEINS, substances that provide the material for building cells. There are thousands of different proteins in cells and each carries out a particular job. For instructions to be issued, part of the DNA molecule must unwind to expose the chemical code on its rungs. The code is copied and the copy leaves the nucleus. The cell is then instructed to make a particular protein.

There are several lengths of DNA inside a cell's nucleus. (Interestingly, only 1 percent of the DNA in a human cell is used to control its activities. The rest is redundant.) Each length is combined with other substances to form a CHROMOSOME. DNA is folded up into the chromosome very tightly indeed.

A CHROMOSOME MAY BE 10,000 TIMES SHORTER THAN THE LENGTH OF DNA IT CONTAINS • DNA IS MADE UP FROM SMALLER MOLECULES • DNA IS MADE UP FROM SMALLER MOLECULES • A CHROMOSOME MAY BE 100,000 GENES, HUMANS 100,000 GENES • FRUITFLIES HAVE AROUND 5,000 GENES, HUMANS 100,000 GENES • FRUITFLIES HAVE AROUND THE EARTH 100,000 TIMES • TO GO AROUND THE EARTH 100,000 TIMES

DNA MAKES COPIES OF ITSELF

1 Each strand with its sequence of rungs provides instructions for the creation of new DNA

2 DNA "unzips" itself

3 A new strand is made by copying the sequence of rungs

MOLECULE

BEFORE us lies a mass of different colored beads. Each color represents a different sort of atom. On this illustration, red is for oxygen atoms, blue for nitrogen, white for hydrogen, yellow for phosphorus, and green for carbon. The atoms are clustered together. Some are squashed against each other.

Groups of atoms like this are called molecules. DNA is a giant molecule. The atoms illustrated here are just a very few of the millions it contains. The DNA giant molecule is itself made up of many smaller molecules. The smaller molecules, of which there are a number of different types, each have their own special pattern of atoms.

On with our journey. We'll aim for one of those green carbon atoms. We must shrink still further to enter yet another new world...

MANY OF THE MOLECULES IN LIVING THINGS DO NOT EXIST AT ALL IN THE NONLIVING WORLD • CARBON-BASED

DNA IS A CARBON-BASED MOLECULE • DNA IS A CARBON-BASED MOLECULE

THERE ARE AT LEAST TEN THOUSAND DIFFERENT KINDS OF MOLECULE IN THE HUMAN BODY •

GAS (e.g. STEAM)

Molecules are fast-moving and widely separated

SOLID (e.g. ICE)

Molecules are packed together in a regular arrangement

LIQUID (e.g. WATER)

Molecules are slow-moving and quite close together

MOLECULE

WHEN ATOMS ARE JOINED together by strong chemical bonds (☞ ATOM) they form MOLECULES. In some cases, a molecule is formed from two or more atoms of the same type. For example, a molecule of oxygen gas (written in chemical shorthand as O_2) contains two atoms of oxygen. There are a great many examples of molecules containing two or more atoms of different kinds. A molecule of water (H_2O), for instance, contains two hydrogen atoms and one oxygen atom. A molecule of carbon dioxide (CO_2) contains one carbon atom and two oxygen atoms.

Living things contain tens of thousands of different molecules of various shapes and sizes. The most abundant molecule in living things, and one of the simplest, is water. The largest is *deoxyribonucleic acid* (DNA for short). Many of the larger and more important molecules in living things contain the element carbon.

A giant molecule like DNA is formed by combining together smaller molecules. In DNA, these molecules join together to form two very long chains.

The common chemical ELEMENTS in the bodies of animals and plants are all present in the air or the rocks which make up the Earth's crust (☞ LAND). What is special is the way these elements are combined as molecules inside living things. These molecules work together to repair and maintain all working parts of a living thing, and to produce offspring in the same form.

THERE ARE AS MANY MOLECULES IN A TEASPOON OF WATER AS THERE ARE TEASPOONS OF WATER IN THE ATLANTIC OCEAN

MOLECULES ARE MADE UP OF ATOMS • MOLECULES ARE MADE UP OF ATOMS

ALL THE OTHER ELEMENTS PUT TOGETHER • MOLECULES OUTNUMBER TENFOLD THOSE OF

CARBON AND THE MOLECULES OF LIFE
Combines with other atoms to make living matter

CARBON HAS DIFFERENT FORMS
Graphite soft (weak bonds), diamond hard (strong bonds)

Makes rings: e.g. benzene (important industrial chemical)

Makes chains: e.g. methane (1 carbon atom), octane (8)

CARBON CAN MAKE STABLE BONDS WITH ITSELF

A TOM

THIS *is an illustration of the inside of a carbon atom. The cross-section, actually measuring a few thousandths of a millionth of an inch across, fills the circular shape exactly. The inside of the atom is an almost completely empty space except for a tiny body in the center and six points of fizzing energy hurtling incessantly around it. On this illustration, the central body, or atomic nucleus, is drawn much larger than in its real proportions, just so we can see it at all. With its closely packed red and black "beads," representing protons and neutrons respectively, the nucleus resembles a raspberry.*

The six fizzing bodies are electrons. They race around ceaselessly, four tracing a pattern in the outer shell, the other two confined to the inner shell.

We head for the center. Surely this our journey's end, the smallest part of all matter? Not quite...

IF A NUCLEUS WAS A GOLF BALL IN THE CENTER OF A STADIUM, THE EDGE OF TH

ATOMS BOND TOGETHER TO FORM MOLECULES • ATOMS BOND TOGETHER TO FORM MOLECULES • ATOMS BOND TOGETHER TO FORM MOLECULES

THE NUCLEUS IS 100,000 TIMES SMALLER THAN THE WHOLE ATOM •

• SSOADA HONI NA NI HTNOILLIM A FO SHTDNASUOHT RUOF TUOBA SI MOTA NEGORDYH A

ELEMENTS HAVE DIFFERENT NUMBERS OF ELECTRONS AND PROTONS IN THEIR ATOMS

The sun is mostly made of hydrogen

Lead is used to make shot gun pellets

Neon is used to make electric lights

BAR

Sulfur is found in egg yolks

Silver is used to make jewelry

ELEMENTS HAVE DIFFERENT NUMBERS OF ELECTRONS AND PROTONS IN THEIR ATOMS

Calcium is found in chalk, milk, and bones

ATOM

ALL SUBSTANCES are composed from 92 naturally occurring ELEMENTS and an ATOM is the smallest part of an element that can exist. Atoms are so small that the full-stop at the end of this sentence contains more than *one billion* of them.

Tiny as it is, an atom is almost entirely made up of empty space. The rest consists of protons, neutrons and ELECTRONS. Protons and neutrons are found clustered together in a minute, extremely dense nucleus at the very centre of the atom. Little bundles of energy called electrons whizz around this nucleus at the speed of light. It is the presence of electrons that make the atom behave like a solid, in the same way that a fan blade spinning rapidly looks and behaves as if it were solid.

In an atom there are the same number of electrons as there are protons. Both have electrical charges: electrons negative, protons positive. Unlike charges attract, and so the atom is held together. Each of the 92 elements has a different number of electrons and protons in their atoms.

Electrons bond one atom to another to make MOLECULES. When two atoms share a pair of electrons this forms a *covalent bond*. When an electron leaves one atom and enters another, the two atoms become IONS held together by an *ionic bond*. Other types of bond include *metallic bonds,* in which the outer electrons float around in a common pool, and *hydrogen bonds* found between water molecules, in which positively charged hydrogen atoms are attracted to negatively charged oxygen atoms.

THE GREEK PHILOSOPHER DEMOCRITUS (460-400 BC) WAS THE FIRST TO SUGGEST THAT MATTER WAS MADE UP OF TINY PARTICLES

PROTONS AND NEUTRONS ARE MADE UP OF PARTICLES

PROTONS ARE ABOUT 2,000 TIMES HEAVIER THAN ELECTRONS

PROTONS WOULD BE THE STADIUM'S OUTER WALL

ATOMS BOND IN DIFFERENT WAYS

A hydrogen bond between water molecules

An ionic bond between sodium and chlorine ions

In a metallic bond outer electrons move around freely

Covalent bond between hydrogen and oxygen atoms (water)

ATOMS BOND IN DIFFERENT WAYS

PARTICLE

EVEN the protons and neutrons packed together in the miniscule nucleus of an atom contain something else! Each no more than one hundredth of a billion billionth of an inch across, these subatomic particles are known as quarks. Nobody, however, can say what a quark looks like because nobody has ever seen one.

In this illustration, the quarks are represented by balls, colored white for "up" quarks and blue for "down" quarks—simply the names given to two sorts of quark that behave in different ways. The small golden balls represent gluons, whose function is to bond or "glue" the quarks together.

Our journey has reached the limit of human knowledge. But maybe we could go on and travel deep inside the quarks themselves. What other strange, new worlds might we find there..?

THE NAME QUARK • MORE THAN 200 KINDS OF SUBATOMIC PARTICLES HAVE NOW BEEN DISCOVERED •

ATOMS ARE MADE UP OF PARTICLES • ATOMS ARE MADE UP OF PARTICLES • THE NUCLEUS OF A HYDROGEN ATOM IS ABOUT A MILLION-BILLIONTH OF A FOOT ACROSS •

NUCLEAR FUSION

This is fairly similar to the way that the Sun produces energy 1 Two hydrogen nuclei smash together 2 They combine to form a helium nucleus 3 A neutron is released, together with large amounts of energy

1
1
2
3

NUCLEAR FUSION

PARTICLE

THE ATOM is the smallest part of a substance. But an atom is not the smallest thing there is. Inside an atom are even smaller, SUBATOMIC PARTICLES. Most of these are crammed into the tiny nucleus at the center of the atom (the other subatomic particles are ELECTRONS ☞ ATOM). Particles with a positive electrical charge, called *protons*, and neutral particles, called *neutrons*, jostle for space inside the atom's minute nucleus.

A very powerful force keeps these two kinds of particles together. It is called the *strong nuclear force* and operates at the tiny distances found within the nucleus.

Incredibly, protons and neutrons are themselves formed from still smaller particles, called *quarks*. Protons and neutrons both contain three quarks, but they contain a different balance of two kinds of quark, known as "up" or "down." Neutrons contain one up quark and two down quarks, while protons contain two up quarks and one down quark. Protons can readily change into neutrons, and vice versa, by changing one of their quarks.

The strong nuclear force of the nucleus is carried by other subatomic particles, called *gluons,* which lie among the quarks. When nuclei collide and join together *(nuclear fusion)*, as happens in the Sun (☞ SOLAR SYSTEM), the strong nuclear force is released as massive amounts of energy. Nuclear energy can also be released when atomic nuclei are split apart. This process is called *nuclear fission:* it is used in nuclear power stations.

PHYSICISTS DISTINGUISH BETWEEN THE 18 KINDS OF QUARK BY THEIR DIFFERENT "COLORS" AND "FLAVORS" • NAM-LLEG YARRUM TSICISYHP NACIREMA EHT YB DESU DROW ESNESNON A SAW

NUCLEAR FISSION

1 A neutron smashes into nucleus of a uranium atom 2 Nucleus splits in two 3 Neutrons are released, together with large amounts of energy 4 The released neutrons blast into other uranium atomic nuclei

NUCLEAR FISSION

THE INCREDIBLE JOURNEY TO THE EDGE OF THE UNIVERSE

TAKE ANY OBJECT: a chair, an insect, or even just the air around us. You may already know that all these are made up of minute particles called atoms. But did you know that atoms themselves are also made up of particles? They are so small that scientists cannot see them, even through the most powerful of microscopes. But they are the tiny building blocks from which the entire Universe is made.

If particles come together, they make atoms. If atoms join up, molecules are produced. The organs essential to life are made of molecules. Animals, plants, and other forms of life share the planet Earth, itself one of the Sun's family of planets. And the Sun is one star in the Milky Way Galaxy—just one galaxy in billions that make up the Universe.

This book takes you on a journey of exploration through the Universe...

BARNES
&NOBLE
BOOKS
NEW YORK